STARLA YILMAZ

The Butterfly Wisdom

TAROT

Guiding Wings for Your Journey

REDFeather™

MIND | BODY | SPIRIT

4880 Lower Valley Road, Atglen, PA 19310

Dedicated to all searching for comfort during their metamorphosis.

Designed by Alexa Harris
Cover design by Brenda McCallum
Type set in Daydreamer/AdvertRough-Two/Griffith Gothic
ISBN: 978-0-7643-6923-0
Printed in China

Published by REDFeather Mind, Body, Spirit
An imprint of Schiffer Publishing, Ltd.
4880 Lower Valley Road
Atglen, PA 19310
Phone: (610) 593-1777; Fax: (610) 593-2002
Email: Info@redfeathermbs.com
Web: www.redfeathermbs.com

MIX
Paper | Supporting
responsible forestry
FSC® C020560

For our complete selection of fine books on this and related subjects, please visit our website at www.redfeathermbs.com. You may also write for a free catalog.

REDFeather Mind, Body, Spirit's titles are available at special discounts for bulk purchases for sales promotions or premiums. Special editions, including personalized covers, corporate imprints, and excerpts, can be created in large quantities for special needs. For more information, contact the publisher.

Table of Contents

Acknowledgments..4

Introduction...5

Using This Deck......................................7

Major Arcana 13

Minor Arcana 58

    Swords...59

    Wands 76

    Cups.. 92

    Disks.. 111

Healing Patterns and Prompts.............129

Recommended Resources.....................142

Acknowledgments

To my husband, my star in the sky. For always standing next to me.

To Replacement Units One and Two, my honey heart and my joy. For giving my days color and life.

To Mom, for teaching me how to sew.

To Dad, for always forcing me to finish what I start.

To Nonnie, for showing me how to cross-stitch.

To Sara Beth Shepheard, for introducing me to Tarot decades ago.

To Alicia May Vamvoukakis, for creating *The Embroidered Graveyard Oracle*. It is truly a special deck.

To Deborah Blake, for your mentorship on this project. Your guidance was invaluable.

To Dr. Jeffrey Vasseur, for teaching me the art of the short story. You really were a great teacher. I hope one of these microfictions is "good," although Chekhov would say I need to write a few more before asking his opinion on them.

Thank you all.

Introduction

Soon after an intense healing phase of my life, I had a vision. Butterflies cross-stitched onto white canvas, each one the focus of a Tarot card, forming one giant tapestry. Once my eyes cleared and the real world returned, I laughed.

A cross-stitcher for most of my life, I knew the amount of work that project would entail. Besides, I had never once considered myself an artist. I was a writer. When I did work on a craft, I simply followed a pattern. The butterflies in my vision would have to be something I drew and designed. I had zero confidence I could even hope to approach the beauty seen in my vision.

So I ignored it and kept working on my writing projects. I was hopeful for them, but after a couple of months, my writing projects imploded and I found my writing self shattered. That's when the vision returned. This time, I picked up a needle.

Each stitch pulled those slivers of myself back together, and my confidence grew as the butterflies multiplied. As it healed me, I could feel that healing energy transferring into the fabric itself. And if these butterflies had healed me, then surely they would heal others.

But I still did not understand why the vision had come to me. After all, many people knew more about Tarot than I did, were better artists than I was, and were better stitchers than I am.

When I consulted other decks with this question, I found the answers confusing. Lots of Wands and the Hierophant continued to show up. Gifts of literary-themed Tarot decks began appearing in my life when I had spent over two decades reading privately with three much-loved decks. Cards featuring scribes of pens and quills began flying out of those decks when I shuffled them.

Ignoring these confusing messages, I started working on the guidebook. Initially, I wrote it as a typical guidebook, with detailed explanations of the artwork and the meaning of the cards. But I found that process and its result as dull as dried concrete. Also, it was doing nothing to heal that writer within me.

I tried multiple different ways of structuring the guidebook before I settled on microfictions. Humans are storytelling creatures, and I hope that these very short stories not only make the reader contemplate their meaning instead of reciting keywords but will also aid the newer Tarot reader in remembering each card's meaning. I believe that those microfictions combined with the cross-stitch and my familiarity with Tarot are why the vision came to me. Moreover, writing in this way added the final piece to my healing puzzle.

I know some people will struggle to find the meaning in short stories, so I have included the Key Ideas, which are all many people will need. The "Thoughts for Deeper Interpretation" sections are there for those who are still exploring the meaning of their reading. I hope at least one of the three will show the reader, through the cards, the meaningful answer to their questions and feel like a gentle hug during challenging times.

After the guidebook portion of this book, I have included several patterns and writing prompts for you, Reader, to partake of the healing yourself. While the patterns have both an advanced and beginner option, the writing prompts work for whatever level of writer you are. I hope that these tools will aid you on your healing journey. As a reminder, they are not a replacement for a medical doctor or licensed therapist but are meant to work in conjunction with those professionals.

Using This Deck

There is no right or wrong way to use Tarot, but here are my recommendations. As with any magical tool, the first step is to connect with it. Some people put a new deck under their pillow and sleep a night before attempting their first reading. Others keep it on their altar for a while. Another option is to go through every single card and examine each card's artwork. Or you can open the deck and jump into your first question.

There are a multitude of other options, but whichever you choose will be the best way to introduce yourself to your deck. I like to leaf through each card in a new deck and see what feelings the artwork inspires in me. I also like to read through the guidebook to explore the author's intention with each card's meaning.

After introducing myself to the deck, I will shuffle it four times, divide it into six piles, and then shuffle those piles individually before recombining them and shuffling the deck four more times. Once I'm satisfied the cards have been sufficiently randomized, then I will do my first reading.

I like to do a deck introduction spread, which will be included later in this section. What's important is that you find one you are comfortable with and that works for you. Following are several different types of readings that I hope will benefit you on your Tarot-reading journey.

With all of that being said, let's get into a sample of the different types of readings you can do.

One Card

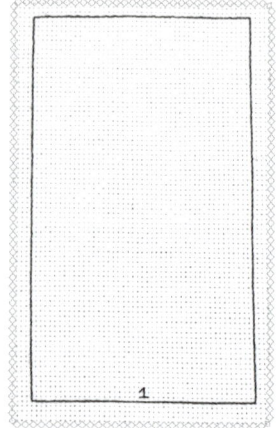

A one-card drawing is the simplest form of Tarot reading you can do. It also needs very little explanation. Ask a question, shuffle, and draw a card. Depending on your question, however, you may find one card an unsatisfactory answer due to the limited nature of a single card. This simple spread, though, is perfect for a quick reading. Also, if you are new to Tarot, drawing a card a day is an excellent way to learn the meanings of the cards.

Three Card

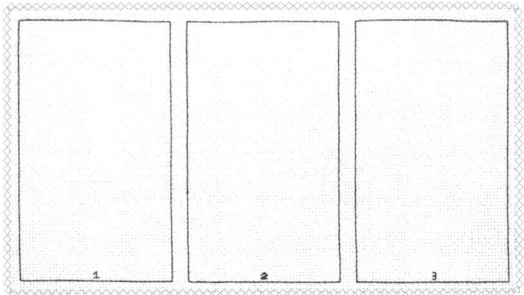

If you are looking for a more detailed answer, then three cards is a good reading to do that is still fairly simple to understand. Again, ask your question and shuffle the cards. Make sure you have the type of reading in mind as you shuffle. Once you feel that the cards are ready, draw three cards. Here are different examples of three-card readings you could do:

PAST, PRESENT, FUTURE

1. Past—This card represents what had previously happened that has led up to the current situation.
2. Present—This card shows what is currently happening in your situation.
3. Future—This card gives a glimpse into how the situation resolves, assuming nothing changes. As always, the future will change on the basis of every decision we and others make.

SITUATION, ACTION, OUTCOME

1. Situation—This is an overview of the situation as it stands now.
2. Action—This card represents what action the cards suggest you take.
3. Outcome—Given card 1 and if you do as card 2 suggests, then this is the likely result of your current situation and the given action.

YOU, YOUR PARTNER, YOUR RELATIONSHIP

1. You—This card is about your place in this relationship.
2. Your Partner—This one describes the role your partner plays.
3. Your Relationship—This card describes the current status of your relationship.

If you want more details regarding what action to take to impact card 3, do another reading (such as Situation, Action, Outcome).

Four Card

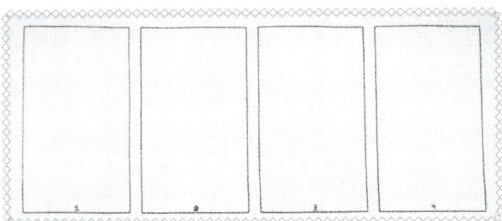

These spreads are useful for getting information on different facets of a situation. As always, feel free to improvise and come up with your own card combinations once you become familiar with the Tarot. One type of question that is traditionally difficult to answer is yes/no questions, but I have developed and included a spread that I find helpful for those.

YES/NO

One of the easiest types of questions to ask, but a challenging one for the cards to answer. This spread provides a yes or no answer and then provides deeper meaning into that answer.
1. The Answer—Interpreting this depends on the other cards, but basically if this card trumps the other three, then your answer is a simple yes. The card itself will provide a deeper explanation of that yes or no.
2. Past—Past events that influenced the situation
3. Present—Present events that are currently unfolding
4. Action—Suggested action to take. This is highly open to interpretation depending on whether you want the answer to stay as yes or no.

DECK INTRODUCTION

I find it useful with a new deck to let the deck introduce itself to me.

1. Strengths as a deck
2. Weaknesses as a deck
3. What are you here to teach me?
4. The potential outcome of our collaboration

PARTS OF YOU

I like to use this spread to check in and see how the different parts of myself are doing. These are how I usually see myself, but please feel free to adjust for yourself as necessary.

1. How I am as a parent.
2. How I am as a romantic partner.
3. How I am at work.
4. How I am as an artist.

Major
Arcana

1–The Magician

KEY IDEAS
willpower, skill, potential, resourcefulness,
creativity, action

A peacock butterfly watched a Magician use a wand to create an entire universe in his hands the size of a ball. Wishing to juggle the heavens in the same way, that night as the Magician slept, the butterfly stole the Magician's wand. She stroked the carved symbols, sword, cup, pentacle, wand, and infinity, with her forelegs. Then, she drew in power through the wand and created her own universes, one after another, until she had seventy-eight with which to juggle.

Then the wand shattered. The butterfly mourned her loss, thinking she had lost the power to create forever. The Magician woke. When he saw what the butterfly had done, he laughed. He explained that the power had not come from the wand, but from the butterfly herself, and that all had the same infinite power to create inside them. You needed only your willpower and skill to wield it. The butterfly dried her eyes and reached for the power. She laughed as once again she flew among seventy-eight universes.

Thoughts for Deeper Interpretation

What skills do you have that could aid your situation?

How can you release or unlock your power?

Are there other areas that your skills can transfer over to?

2—The High Priestess

KEY IDEAS
wisdom, hidden knowledge, intuition,
mysteries and secrets

The holly blue butterfly visited a temple to sit on the crescent moon arch, bask in the sun, and listen to the High Priestess share her wisdom. That's when the men attacked the temple. The High Priestess had no chance. They stabbed her through the chest and ripped her book off the altar.

When they realized that her book held only gibberish for them, they threw it on the marble floor and left bloody boot prints on its pages. Their duty completed, the men left the High Priestess to die alone.

The holly blue butterfly flew down to offer her one last kiss. Before she could land, the High Priestess stood. Red spread through her robes as she picked up the book and lay it back on the altar. Then, she turned to the butterfly.

"You are the High Priestess now." She fell.

The butterfly almost flew away and left the unwanted bloody legacy behind. But the book fluttered open in a sudden breeze, an invitation she could not fly past. She landed on the open page and began to read. The book's secrets poured into her, igniting a deep intuitive power she didn't know she had.

Thoughts for Deeper Interpretation

Do you think you are the high priestess or the butterfly, and why?
Is there a power of your own you are not utilizing?
What knowledge do you think the universe's book might hold for you?

3—The Empress

KEY IDEAS
abundance, feminine wisdom and power,
fertility, mother, commitment

A monarch butterfly flew over a desert. Exhausted, she searched for a suitable place to land and lay her eggs. After miles of flying, she finally found a ruin crumbling to dust. In its center lay a crown, which encircled a solitary yellow milkweed plant. With gratitude in her heart, the monarch finally landed.

The ground had just enough moisture under the milkweed and enough nectar in the flowers for her to eat and drink her fill. After she finished, she noticed that the damp sand had spread. Satisfied, she lay her twelve eggs on each of the crown's stars. She almost flew off, then, as was her nature, but worldly feminine power surged through her, and she wondered how else she could transform the area before her brood hatched.

Four days later, the caterpillars emerged to plenty of water and a second milkweed plant that had grown. None of the Empress's progeny ever thirsted or hungered so long as they lay their eggs on the crown's stars.

Thoughts for Deeper Interpretation

How are you like the Empress?

What does worldly feminine power look like to you?

Where in your life could you bless yourself with the Empress's gifts?

4—The Emperor

KEY IDEAS
discipline, stability, self-control, authority

When the monarch butterfly emerged from his chrysalis, he learned that his father, the Emperor, had been murdered, and his killer sat in a cell. After ascending to the throne, which dug into his back and prevented any comfortable slouching, he commanded his court to bring the killer to him.

It didn't take long for them to bring the killer and shove him into the dirt beneath the Emperor's feet. They had crushed the killer's delicate wings; he would never fly again. They had ripped off one antenna; he had no hope of escaping predators. They had bent his proboscis; he would not live much longer.

No pity touched the Emperor as he considered how he would like to exercise his authority over the crippled butterfly killer.

Thoughts for Deeper Interpretation

What should the Emperor do with the killer?
How could you exercise self-control?
Where in your life do you think you could use more discipline?

5—The Hierophant

KEY IDEAS
conformity, structured learning, tradition, religion, academia, teaching

A large white butterfly initially went to school for computer programming. However, in his sophomore year, he had a vision: He flew over thousands of gathered caterpillars and butterflies with St. Peter's crossed keys shimmering in the air. The next day he left the university and enrolled in seminary school.

The path challenged his willpower every day. When he saw his university friends smiling and partying while he sipped on water, he asked himself why he flew this path. When he sat as a guest at their weddings, while he had vowed to have no life partner, he asked why he flew this path. And when he toured their fine houses bought with the salary he could have had, he asked himself why he flew this path.

The vision, however, would not let him stray. And when he finally flew over two caterpillar acolytes and saw the crossed keys in the air, he understood all.

Thoughts for Deeper Interpretation

Is there a field of study you have always wanted to pursue? Maybe now is the time.

What would it look like if you were to mentor someone, and what do you think you might learn by doing so?

Whatever your religious beliefs are now, what childhood religious traditions could aid you and your situation?

6—The Lovers

KEY IDEAS
love, attraction, partnership, communication, sex,
relationship, duality, decision, choice

A New Zealand red admiral butterfly prayed for his perfect partner. The next day, he met two butterflies and fell in love with both. However, the women did not love each other, and jealousy began to chip away at their hearts.

One retreated to flirt with other butterflies, saying he knew where to find her when he was ready to put her first. The other shadowed his every wing beat and threatened to drown herself if he did not choose her.

Another prayer told him the one to marry. But which?

Thoughts for Deeper Interpretation

Is there a quality you need to work on to be a better partner?

What do you think healthy love looks like?

Which butterfly do you think answered the prayer, and why?

7—The Chariot

KEY IDEAS
overcoming conflict or obstacles, moving forward in a
positive direction, ambition, drive, holding on to two
opposing forces

A large tree nymph heard that the king's guard had an opening, a position that came with a pay raise and a golden laurel wreath. Others volunteered as well—his competition—and all of them were directed inside an arena. They lined up in the sand, under the king hovering above.

"You all are brave, but that is not enough. Only one of you will join the ranks of those at my side, protecting me. In a moment, a pair of sphinxes will enter the arena. Whichever one of you can take hold of the pair's reins and drive them across the city to my palace first will become the newest member of my guard and receive a golden laurel wreath."

Nervous wings twitched as a gate opened and the sphinxes stepped toward the assembled butterflies. The large tree nymph approached first. Hissing, a sphinx swiped with large claws. The butterfly dodged, but a blow from behind shoved the nymph into the sand.

As chaos erupted in the butterfly ranks, the sphinxes purred. The nymph shook its head and took to the air. With perfectly timed and placed blows, the nymph slipped unnoticed through the sand. Again, he approached the sphinxes and bowed, asking, "May I take your reins?"

The sphinxes did not nod, but they didn't hiss either. The nymph picked up the reins and the sphinxes sprang forward, pulling the nymph along as they drove toward the golden laurel wreath of victory.

Thoughts for Deeper Interpretation

What does victory look like to you?

How long can you hold on to two opposing forces?

Where are the universe's sphinxes leading you?

8—Strength

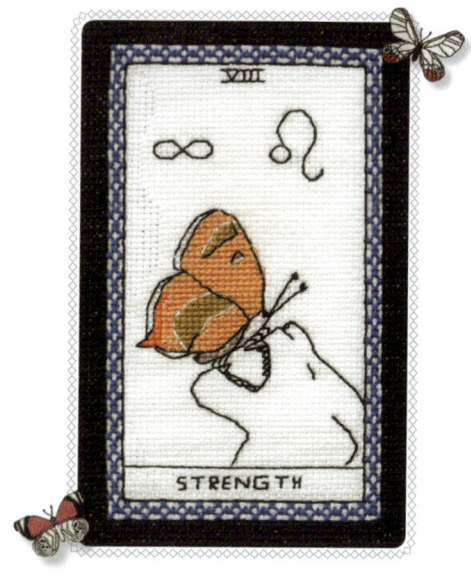

KEY IDEAS
physical strength, mental/emotional strength, compassion,
confidence, courage, integrity, control

A brown hairstreak liked to fly and enjoy the sun. One day, a roar echoed over the land. Curious, the butterfly fluttered down to investigate. After searching the savanna below, she found a lioness rolling on the ground and pawing at her mouth.

"Are you all right?" the butterfly asked the lioness. She stopped roaring and stood to narrow her eyes at the butterfly. "Thank god! A bit of bone got stuck in my teeth and pains me. Could you pull it out? Please?"

Now, the idea of crawling into a lion's mouth terrified the butterfly, but seeing the lioness's misery broke the butterfly's heart, and compassion overruled her fear. The butterfly swallowed and nodded. "All right. Open wide."

And into the cavern of sharp fangs and canines the butterfly went. There, deep in the back of the mouth, stuck between two teeth and glinting red in the dark, was the bone shard.

"Hold still," the butterfly said and began to pull. A growl rumbled from the lioness's throat, but the jaws did not move. The bone shard popped free, the lioness roared, and the butterfly tumbled into the sun's bright light.

"At last, it's gone! Oh, little butterfly, where are you? Are you hurt?" the lioness roared out. The butterfly righted itself and spread her wings. There were a few missing scales, but she could still fly.

"I'm here and I'm fine."

"Thank you," the lioness said and bowed low before the brown hairstreak.

Thoughts for Deeper Interpretation

What opportunities for growth could be coming out of this ending?

Sometimes we must embrace the dark to be reborn. Is there anything holding you back from doing so, and why?

How else could you prepare for the transformation unfolding in your life?

9—The Hermit

THE HERMIT

KEY IDEAS
solitude, withdrawal, looking inward for answers, self-
discovery, inner reflection

An Old World swallowtail woke to find itself on a mountainside as night began to fall.

"What am I doing here?" he asked as a light appeared in front of him.

"Come," the light said and began to move up the mountain. He followed. It grew darker around them, and echoes began to reach him. Screams. Pleas for help. Sobs.

"What is happening out there in the dark?" he asked.

"With no light to guide them, they became lost."

"Can I be their light?"

"That is why I chose you. This way," she said and moved up the mountain. At the top, an empty lantern glinted. He flew closer. The door opened and she waited behind him. With a nod, he flew inside. She closed the door and faded away. The lantern amplified his light and illuminated the mountaintop.

Thoughts for Deeper Interpretation

How could you go inward to make your light shine brighter?

What does a journey of self-discovery look like to you?

Does the idea of unplugging from screens for a weekend seem impossible? Why or why not, and do you think you could learn anything by doing so?

10—Wheel of Fortune

KEY IDEAS
new direction, fate, luck, destiny, change
(especially in one's fortune)

The peacock pansy never thought about fate or changing fortune until the storm hit. Blue, yellow, and orange lightning flashed all around her like a cage. Trembling, she squeezed her eyes shut and missed witnessing the portal opening. She did feel it, though, as the air spun and pulled her forward.

Her wings and legs stretched away from her thorax as though someone had decided to rip them off. The pain lasted but an instant before ending. All her limbs were intact, and the air stilled. Still trembling, she opened her eyes.

Before her, a stationary wheel hung in the sky with all the stages of her life carved into it. A crack ran down its middle. Blue, yellow, and orange lightning flashed from the wound. She knew how to fix the wheel. Bracing herself, she flew forward. This time, she kept her eyes open. She felt no pain as she joined the wheel and closed in on herself. The lightning stopped. She began to turn.

Thoughts for Deeper Interpretation

What cycle could be coming to an end in your situation?

Is there another direction you could choose to go that might change things for you?

Did luck or fate bring the butterfly to the wheel? Why?

11—Justice

KEY IDEAS
balance, justice, reaping what you sow,
impartiality, fairness, truth

A banded peacock liked to flit among the decaying statues in a forgotten garden. Her favorite was of one holding a set of balanced scales in the left hand and an upright sword in the right. One morning, a man dragged a crying girl into the garden.

She twisted out of his grip and tried to run, but he caught her and slammed her against the statute. The scales tipped and the sword began to lean. As the man ripped at the girl's clothes, the butterfly made its move and landed on the stone blade. Below, the girl laughed.

Confused, he looked up as the sword smashed into his face.

She screamed again, but this time nothing stopped her from running out of the garden. As his last breath sputtered out, the butterfly fluttered over to the scales. The bottom of their basins were still moist with dew. She drank and the scales tipped back into balance.

Thoughts for Deeper Interpretation

In what ways could you bring balance to your situation?

How could examining the situation impartially aid you?

Where do you think you might be lacking truth and fairness in the way you are approaching your situation?

12—The Hanged One

KEY IDEAS
patience, sacrifice, resting before change, short-term loss for
long-term gain, new perspective

Usually, after eight weeks of life, the blue morpho caterpillar turns light green as it prepares to enter the pupa stage. Three days later, it will find a suitable twig or large leaf to attach itself to and rest for thirty-six to forty-eight hours. During this time, the chrysalis begins to grow beneath its skin. When ready, the skin will split, like someone unzipping a coat, to reveal what looks like a small, green conch shell. It sits there for a least two weeks before the blue morpho butterfly emerges.

Thoughts for Deeper Interpretation

What is a different way to examine your situation?

Are there any mindsets or ways of thinking that aren't serving your situation and could benefit you by sacrificing them?

If you are struggling to see your progress, take a moment to breath and compare your situation to where you were a year ago. Five years ago. Now do you see how far you have come?

13—Death

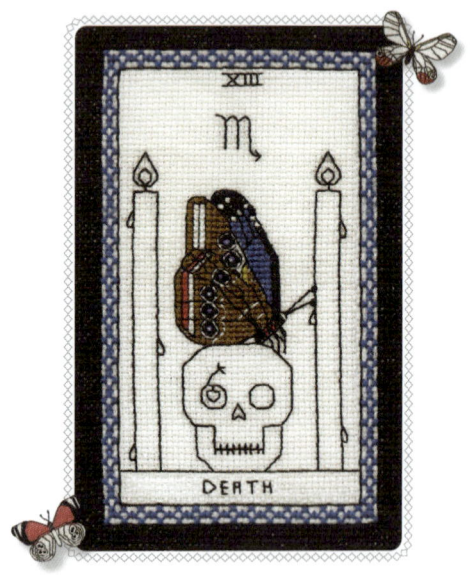

KEY IDEAS
endings, loss, rebirth, change, transformation,
depression, renewal

The blue morpho caterpillar lived a normal life until it came time to transition into a chrysalis. With his green skin hardening, he searched for a leaf or twig to attach himself to, but he found only bones. He tried to hold off the transformation, but change is inevitable. With no other option, he hung himself from a skull's eye socket. He knew his time had come.

His chrysalis hardened, his skin fell away, and his body began to dissolve as the metamorphosis began. That's when Death's energy began to fill him. You see, a mortal form cannot personify a concept forever, and when that form dies, the concept must find a new host. And while Death knew that this butterfly form would not last, he needed to know the life of every being it took. Besides, there is no comparison to feeling himself lifted into the air and seeing people greet him with smiles instead of screams.

Thoughts for Deeper Interpretation

What opportunities for growth could be coming out of this ending?

Sometimes we must embrace the dark to be reborn. Is there anything holding you back from doing so, and why?

How else could you prepare for the transformation unfolding in your life?

14—Temperance

KEY IDEAS
moderation, mixing two discordant elements, harmony, compromise, healing

A thirsty Godart's *Agrias* came across two cups. Curious, they landed on the rim of one and found it full of red liquid. They tasted it, and the saccharine syrup overpowered them and made them gag. The other cup held a blue liquid whose acrid vinegar made the butterfly choke.

Who could drink from either cup?

Still thirsty, the butterfly used what strength they had to tip the cups over. The red and blue liquids combined and bubbled before turning clear. Then, the butterfly drank their fill of the pure water, mindful to leave plenty for those who would follow them.

Thoughts for Deeper Interpretation

Is there something you need to compromise on but don't want to?
Where do you see yourself needing moderation?
How could you bring two disparate elements of your life together?

15—The Devil

KEY IDEAS

ambition, temptation, addiction, feeling imprisoned,
hedonism, greed, obsession, success

An ambitious *Heliconius antiochus* came upon two New Zealand red admiral caterpillars and saw in them a mirror. He fluttered down in front of them and smiled.

"Hello! Do I have a special offer for you!"

"Sorry, we aren't interested," they said and tried to crawl around the butterfly. Anticipating this response, the butterfly's smile did not falter as he said, "I know. You have that test coming up that will determine your future. I can help you pass."

The male caterpillar stopped and turned back to the butterfly. "How?"

With twinkling eyes, the butterfly unspooled a chain with a shackle on one end. "Not only will this accessory enhance physical pleasure, but it will also make all your dreams come true."

While the male caterpillar considered, the female tugged at him. "It's too good to be true, don't you think?"

Ignoring her, the male caterpillar slipped the shackle around him. The butterfly rubbed its forelegs together.

Thoughts for Deeper Interpretation

What could be tempting you right now?

Are there any habits that are keeping you chained and no longer serve you?

Consider the cost of your ambition and weigh whether it truly is worth it.

16—The Tower

KEY IDEAS
ruin, destruction, overthrow, shortsightedness leading to
ruin, unexpected change

Two California sisters each built a tower. One spent time on the foundation, ensuring she had something solid to build on. The other decided to simply build her tower as high as possible, and her tower dwarfed the other. The tall tower's butterfly gloated while the one with the solid foundation shook her head. Both furnished the inside of the towers with rich fabrics and woods.

Then the storm came. Rain pounded, wind lashed, and lightning struck both towers. Flames devoured the insides before the heat made the brick exteriors crumble. When calm skies returned, both towers lay in ruins.

The tall one's butterfly wept, for nothing remained of her tower. However, the one who had spent time on her foundation saw that not only had her foundation escaped unscathed, but her tower's base had survived as well. With gratitude, she lifted her face to the sun before rebuilding her tower.

Thoughts for Deeper Interpretation

Which butterfly do you think you are in your situation?

How do you think you could ensure you have a solid foundation moving forward?

What lessons could you learn from this experience that will aid you in the future?

17—The Star

KEY IDEAS
hope, inspiration, wishes, promise, guidance,
healing, new direction

At dusk, the Florida purplewing liked to sip at the lantana's nectar and watch the constellations come out. One day, a crying woman stumbled outside. The butterfly didn't plan on getting involved—it had been a long day and she wanted to rest, but she paused as the woman sprinkled ashes at the flower's base. When the woman said, "You won't be alone much longer. Mommy's going to join you soon," the butterfly knew she had to do something.

The woman stood. With no hesitation, the butterfly followed, just making it inside the house before the door closed. The woman opened the medicine cabinet and pulled out a bottle. As she turned to select the perfect final accompanying wine, the butterfly landed on the white plastic cap and spread her wings wide.

"What are you doing there?" the woman asked. To answer, the butterfly flew off, through the open kitchen window, and disappeared among the star-filled sky. The woman stared at the billions of twinkling stars before putting the bottle away.

Thoughts for Deeper Interpretation

Where is your guiding light and how could you follow it?

If you are struggling to see hope, ask yourself what you can look forward to tomorrow, whether it relates to your situation or not.

Make a wish upon a star. Now, what is one thing you can do today that gets you a little bit closer to making that wish come true?

18–The Moon

KEY IDEAS
dreams, illusions, unconscious, taming one's animal nature,
cycles, uncertainty

One full-moon night, a luna moth flew at the forest's edge when a dog's barking and yowling shattered the peaceful evening. Concerned that something had injured the dog, the moth changed course and followed the howls deep into the forest. As the dog grew louder, the moth's wing beats grew faster.

Then, the trees parted and revealed a smooth lake that perfectly reflected the moon's face. On the shore stood the dog, growling at the moon's mirrored image. The moth almost laughed, but instead she shook her head and flew over to the dog. He snapped at her when she tried to meet his eyes.

Taking a deep breath, she flew back and winged over the water. Once in the moon's center, she trailed her tail in the water. The reflection shattered. The dog stopped barking. The moth's wing beats echoed across the lake as she flew upward toward the moon.

Thoughts for Deeper Interpretation

Pay attention to your dreams and nightmares. Have you had any recurring themes appear recently? What could that be trying to tell you?

Is there a side of yourself you struggle to control? Now might be the time for deep introspection to see a different way you could attempt to tame this part of yourself.

Why do you think the moth could tell the real moon from the reflection, and the dog could not? How do you think you could use this insight in your situation?

19–The Sun

KEY IDEAS
joy, success, optimism, happiness, health,
vitality, joyfulness

A silvery checkerspot wrote a book. One rainy night, she asked her husband if he would read it. Days later, he said, "I'm sorry, but I am too busy."

So, she revised and edited the book herself. Once again the finished book pleased her, and she emailed it to agents, asking if they would read it. Weeks passed before one foggy morning when the butterfly received a reply.

"I'm sorry, I'm not the right fit for this story."

Again the butterfly edited and revised her book, and the final version pleased her. This time, she sent it to a publisher, her third time asking, "Would you read it?" Months passed. Then, on a sunny afternoon, her cell phone rang.

"Yes, I love it and want to publish it!"

The butterfly leaped into the air and danced among the sunflowers as she imagined the sun's rays kissing her wings.

Thoughts for Deeper Interpretation

What made the butterfly successful in the end?

Have you celebrated your victories recently? If not, perhaps you should.
    If you have, apply those happy memories and emotions to your current situation.

How could you bring the sun's revitalizing energy into your situation?

20–Judgement

KEY IDEAS
victory of life over death, hearing and answering a call,
forgiveness, a reward for past effort, self-judgment

A sylphina angel lay cold on the ground. It did not want to die, but then, few of us do. He'd had a good life, lots of days in the sun sipping nectar, and many of his children had grown and laid their own eggs. How much more in life could he have asked for?

But as he grew colder and darkness crept in at the edges of his vision, he realized he wanted one more day in the sun. With that wish, he closed his eyes. The cold, dark, dreamless sleep lasted a long time.

One day, a horn reverberated through the dark. The butterfly lifted his head. Were his eyes open? He couldn't tell. Again, the horn sounded and light ripped through the darkness. There, in the distance, an angel with a trumpet in one hand waited, with the other hand held out.

However, the light revealed that between the angel and the butterfly lay a treacherous path filled with crags and valleys where birds and lizards waited. The butterfly hesitated. A third time the angel blew the horn, and this time the sun glinted and illuminated a path. The road remained hard, but now the butterfly had no reservations and took wing.

Thoughts for Deeper Interpretation

Did you feel called to do something when you were younger but life got in the way? Now could be the time to resurrect that dead dream.

Conversely, if you have ignored any signs, ask yourself why. What makes following that call so difficult?

Sometimes, it is easier to forgive others and not judge them than it is to offer the same grace to ourselves. How could you stop judging and offer yourself forgiveness? What would that look like?

21—The World

KEY IDEAS
successful outcome, completed cycle, oneness with the
universe, unified truth, understanding the connection
between endings and beginnings

The eighty-eight butterfly clicked refresh on the browser. Her final grades still had not posted. Shaking her head, she closed the browser and flew to work. There, in a corner library office, one of her coworkers greeted her.

"How is our latest graduate doing today?"

"I haven't graduated yet," she said as she clocked in.

"You basically have."

"All depends on my grades. You know that," she said. Her coworker rolled their eyes. "What I know is that the ones who worry whether their grades are good enough or not don't actually have to worry. Now, just relax and enjoy your last day as a work-study student."

"Thanks. I'll try," she promised and looked at the stack of book requests from other libraries. Instead of joining her, her coworker tapped their chin for several seconds. Then their eyes sparkled and they started tapping on their phone.

"I know exactly what you need."

"What's that then?"

Upbeat synth music zipped from the phone's speaker and electrified the air. Her coworker bowed and offered a foreleg. She rolled her eyes but took their foreleg in hers, and they rose into the air and began to dance. When the song ended, she got a text that grades were posted.

"You want to check?" her coworker asked.

"In a minute," she said and continued dancing.

Thoughts for Deeper Interpretation

When did you last dance in the middle of the day for no reason? What would happen if you danced right now?

What wisdom do you think you can carry over from this cycle to the next one?

Think about the lessons this journey taught you. Which one could you share with someone still making their journey?

0–The Fool

KEY IDEAS
beginnings, spontaneity, a leap of faith,
a new journey or life phase, unknown destinations with
dangers or rewards at the end

It was the blue morpho's first flight after emerging from a chrysalis. The air rushing through her wings and over her head, thorax, and legs exhilarated her more than anything she had ever dreamed of as a caterpillar. She never wanted to land.

Sadly, her wings did eventually tire, while thirst and hunger made the rest of her body ache. Her joyful wanderings grew purposeful, and after a few minutes she spotted a flower at the top of a cliff. However, in the distance tiny specks circled.

Birds.

They were far away, though, and surely she could fly fast enough to escape if they did decide to attack, right? Besides, she needed to eat and wanted to get back to her joyful flitting as soon as possible. With that, she flew up the cliff face and headed toward the flower.

Thoughts for Deeper Interpretation

How could you bring in a little bit of forethought as you embark on your next phase of life?

Is there a way to channel some of the Fool's joyous spontaneity into your life or situation right now?

What other lessons do you think the Fool might have to offer you?

Minor
Arcana

SWORDS

Ace of Swords

KEY IDEAS
breakthrough, clear mind, new ideas, cutting through confusion, new beginnings

A golden-banded skipper's office had a problem. His invoicing software and order-tracking software could not connect, which meant that someone, the gold-banded skipper, had to enter the client and order information twice. This not only wasted the skipper's time but also increased the likelihood of an error occurring.

There had to be a better way. But try as he might, the skipper could not get the programs to talk to one another. He then tried to write a script that would pull and import the data from one program to the other, but they even refused that. Clouds of frustration filled his mind and made it impossible for him to think.

Then, like lightning, an idea struck: What if he used a third program to enter in the data and adjusted his script so it would pull the data from the new program and import it into the two existing ones? His forelegs started typing, following the clear line of code laid out in his cloudless mind

2 of Swords

KEY IDEAS
procrastinating making a choice between two undesirable things

An elbowed Pierrot found himself cornered by a wasp and a bird.

"What is this?" the butterfly demanded.

"We both wanted to eat you," the bird said.

"And decided that instead of fighting, we would let you choose," the wasp continued.

The butterfly swallowed. "I don't understand."

The bird laughed. "Come on, it's easy. Do you want me—"

"—or me to eat you?"

The wasp rubbed its legs together, but the butterfly shook her head. "You say it like it's easy, but it is impossible. You both have such beauty. You, bird, with your song and colorful feathers, and you, wasp, with your—"

"Stop delaying. If you can't decide, we will work together and rip you in half," the bird said.

"That isn't fair, is it? I have it on good authority that my right hind wing tastes good only when paired with my left—"

"Enough! Choose!" the wasp demanded. Fear strangled the butterfly's words, and she shrank back from the looming bird and wasp.

Thoughts for Deeper Interpretation

What is holding you back from making this decision?

Not choosing is a choice in itself. What will happen if you continue to ignore what's in front of you?

Who can you turn to for advice in this situation? If you can't think of anyone, you might want to think about reaching out to a therapist or other form of advisor.

3 of Swords

KEY IDEAS
heartbreak, betrayal, sorrow, disintegration

The New Zealand red admiral thought he would be with his partner for the rest of their lives. Perhaps he might have if it weren't for the budget cuts and his partner's subsequent layoff. His partner fell into a depression and refused to leave their branch. The butterfly tried to take care of his partner, but he could do only so much because he had to take on more hours at work to pay the bills.

His partner responded to all of this by refusing to do any housework and sneering that the butterfly wasn't there for him and spent too much time at the office. When the partner finally got a job, the butterfly hoped that things would return to the way they were before. But they didn't.

His partner started working late, and when the butterfly asked what time he would be home, he screamed at him that it was none of their business, and why couldn't they just trust him? His affair and divorce were as cliché as spilled milk, but the unending flow of tears and the pain in his chest that took months to dull was anything but.

Thoughts for Deeper Interpretation

Hugs. How can you offer yourself comfort right now?

Heartbreak doesn't have to involve another person, but the steps to healing are the same. Whom can you reach out to for aid at this moment?

What were the fundamental incompatibilities between you and this person?

4 of Swords

KEY IDEAS
rest, meditation, withdrawal, quieting the mind, relaxation

At night, when the temperature drops, butterflies slip into an inactive, dormant resting mode called a quiescent state. Their eyes remain open and they hide in leaves, bushes, or bark because of the constant predator threat. Often, the butterflies will hang upside down.

One day, as dusk cooled the land, a Tamil lacewing searched for a good leaf to hide under. But humans had cleared the area, and the hiding spaces were either gone or already occupied. The sun dropped below the horizon, and the Tamil lacewing's body began to shut down.

A group of swords proved the only place he could reach. The butterfly did not think he would survive the night, but he had no choice and took hold of one sword, gripping it tightly. As he hung upside down through the night, the sharp, glinting metal deterred all the predators. That night, he rested safer than any night spent among the leaves.

Thoughts for Deeper Interpretation

When did you last take some time to relax?

Do you meditate? If not, maybe now is the time to add that to your routine. If you do, possibly try it a different way, such as using a new visualization or guided sound.

Do you get enough sleep? It's incredibly important to have a healthful sleep routine. If you need to see a doctor about your sleep, do.

5 of Swords

KEY IDEAS
defeat, loss, sorrow, disgrace, humiliation,
victory at another's expense

They were friends as caterpillars, the Sara orange tip and the green hairstreak. At university, they sat next to each other in trigonometry. The Sara orange tip soon showed his natural aptitude, but his surliness kept him from speaking up in class. The green hairstreak, on the other hand, had a hard time with his work but always made the professor smile.

They studied hard over the semester, but at the final, when the green hairstreak held his exam paper, panic overwhelmed him.

He cheated. Number for number, he copied the Sara orange tip's answers. Of course, the teacher noticed that one of them had cheated, and brought them in front of a disciplinary board. The Sara orange tip, insulted by the accusations and process, gave curt, short responses, which the board found rude. The green hairstreak, however, knew how to charm. That made the difference, and they ruled in his favor.

Yet, the victory in his mouth tasted bitter as he watched his former friend, the Sara orange tip, shamed and disgraced, crawl away.

Thoughts for Deeper Interpretation

Is there someone in your life who is taking more than they are giving?
If you are feeling betrayed or taken advantage of, ask yourself if the feeling
is real or coming from something inside yourself.
How could the Sara orange tip move forward from this loss and betrayal?

6 of Swords

KEY IDEAS
giving up, moving on, transitioning, seeking advice or aid

An American copper butterfly closed the doors to her cupcakery for the last time. What kind of bad luck did she have for a celebrity to open a cupcakery of their own a block away from hers? She'd hung on as long as she could, but nothing she tried had stopped the eviction notices from getting taped on her business and apartment doors.

How much farther did she have to fall before she hit rock bottom?

A jingle from her phone paused her tears.

"Hello?" she answered.

"What's wrong?" her best friend asked.

"It's closed," she said.

"I know giving up tastes bitter. Have you thought about applying at that celebrity's cupcakery?"

"How could I go from owning my own business to working for the people who killed my dream?"

"You gotta do what you gotta do. Besides, you might love not having the stress of owning a business."

"I can't think about that right now. Maybe tomorrow, but . . ."

"I feel you. I'll be there soon, and we'll get you through this," her best friend said and hung up. The butterfly should have started walking, but she had more tears to finish shedding first.

7 of Swords

KEY IDEAS
theft, betrayal, trickery, deception

A common bluebottle started stealing as a caterpillar to survive. Food, money, valuables to sell, whatever he could manage to crawl away with, he did. He got caught many times, especially in the beginning, a cycle that only made him better at his illegal profession. The last time, someone helped him get a stable job that supported him, and he no longer needed to steal to live once he became a butterfly.

Yet, his forelegs itched to take that which did not belong to him. Was something broken in his brain? Was it a habit he could not shake? Or was he addicted to the thrill? Whatever the reason, he could resist for only so long.

Of course, the higher in social status he rose, the more options he had that were worth more money. However, he knew that each theft brought him closer to falling into the law's grip. Moreover, some of the tears he saw in his social circle were because he had taken more than a bauble, such as a ring, but someone's heart, smile, or happiness. Even so, he could not stop himself from taking what did not belong to him.

8 of Swords

KEY IDEAS
feeling trapped, blinded, imprisonment, victim mentality, dangerous situation

A small postman butterfly woke to find itself in a cage. At first, she had no fear. She would simply fly through the bars. But when she tried, she found that the cage bars were not wide enough for her wings to fit. Fear began to creep in.

Flying around had made the butterfly hungry and thirsty. That's when she realized there were no flowers, no nectar for her in the cage, and dry sand covered the bottom. She had no food or water. Fear overwhelmed her.

In her panic, she failed to realize that those gaps between the bars, too small for her to fly through, were more than wide enough for her to crawl between on the sand with her wings closed.

Thoughts for Deeper Interpretation

Is there a different way you could examine your situation?

If you are feeling blind, imagine using your other senses to get you through this.

What if you flip the script, and instead of being the victim of a situation, you are a hero overcoming adversity?

9 of Swords

KEY IDEAS
anxiety, despair, worry, overwhelming thoughts, obsession, depression, nightmares

A prey species must always be conscious of its potential predators if it wants to survive. A pipe-vine swallowtail took that concept to the extreme. He could not rest for hearing a wasp buzzing in the leaves. He could not puddle and hydrate himself for feeling a snake sliding across the sand. He could not lap up nectar for seeing a bird flying through the air.

Soon the butterfly grew too weak to spread his wings. His friends tried to encourage him to put his fear to the side, so he could at least do the minimum to survive, but the butterfly could not envision a way around the fear, which coated everything he could see. When the predators finally came, he could do nothing but watch as his fear consumed him.

Thoughts for Deeper Interpretation

Whom could you reach out to for help right now? It is okay to do so. Really. We all need help sometimes. Hugs.

Have you eaten? Slept? Hydrated? Showered? What is something else you could do to take care of yourself today?

Remember, whatever is going on is temporary. You will get through this. Tomorrow is a new day with the potential for miracles to happen. If not tomorrow, then the next day. And so on.

10 of Swords

KEY IDEAS
ruin, painful endings, giving up, surrender, loss

As a caterpillar, a *Callicore aegina* watched the premiere of *Survivor* and fell in love with reality shows. *Big Brother*, *The Challenge*, and more—he devoured them all in equal measure as they came on his TV. It was his dream to be a contestant on one of those shows when he became a butterfly. But while in the chrysalis, something went wrong.

When he emerged as a butterfly, he found himself plagued by random and unpredictable seizures that resisted medication. All his plans and dreams for life were smashed onto the floor.

Some, such as graduating college, he managed to pick the pieces up and glue them back together. Others, such as being on a reality competition show, he had to endure the stinging cuts the pieces inflicted on him as he swept them into the trash.

Thoughts for Deeper Interpretation

The last time you had to give up on something, how did you get through it?
Is there a new opportunity you can look for in this ending?
What can you take away from this situation to help you in the future?

Page of Swords

KEY IDEAS
A new idea or way of communicating has been presented to you, quite possibly by a youth. It is important to spend time analyzing whether this idea is true, practical, and useful before applying it. Pessimism and falsehoods may be present.

A Henry's elfin clutched a fountain pen. Blank parchment stretched in front of him. He had less than twenty-four hours to design a new castle for the king. If the Henry's elfin did not deliver, he would lose his job, and then how would he feed his caterpillar brood? The oldest of said brood crawled up to the butterfly.

"Come see what I made out of blocks," he said. The butterfly lay the pen down and followed his son. Blocks stretched around the couch and rose in the middle of the floor to touch the ceiling fan.

"Daddy, what do you think?"

"It's glorious," the proud butterfly said. He played with his children among the blocks for a while, testing the structural integrity of what they had built. With some modifications, it would do nicely. Once they had moved on from building to smashing, he returned to his pen and parchment.

The next day, the king found the plans satisfactory and ordered construction to begin. The Henry's elfin celebrated by taking his brood for ice cream, with the oldest getting an extra scoop.

Thoughts for Deeper Interpretation

Is there a youth in your life you could spend time with? It might help you gain a fresh perspective on your issue, even if you don't discuss it.

Could pessimism be clouding your analysis of new ideas?

What idea do you need to spend more time examining before implementing it?

Knight of Swords

KEY IDEAS
Ambitious, quick moving, committed to an idea, evidence-based arguments, a protector of intellectual pursuits. There is a younger person in your life who will help you with your idea, whether it be with your commitment or protecting the idea itself. If not, then maybe you need to bring these qualities into your situation.

A purple-and-gold flitter finished donning his armor and took up his sword. Waving it above his head, he shouted, "Tonight we will celebrate your victory!"

His girlfriend simply blinked. "I'm just defending my dissertation."

"Defending, yes! Stand behind me; their attacks will not pierce my armor."

"You know it's an interview, right? Only words. And I'll be on my own."

"I know," the purple-and-gold flitter said. He lowered his sword but did not sheath it.

"You do?" his girlfriend asked with a raised antennae. Smiling, he nodded.

"So why all . . . this?" she asked, waving her wings to indicate his armor and sword.

"To help you visualize," the flitter said. His girlfriend's wings crinkled together in confusion. The flitter nodded.

"When fear begins to consume you, just picture me as I am now, standing between you and your advisors," he explained. A smile spread across her face as understanding dawned. After a kiss, she left to defend her ideas, and he kept his armor on until she texted him that she had passed.

Queen of Swords

KEY IDEAS
Independence, truth seeking, advice, intelligence, getting to the point, sharp tongued, widow. There's someone in your life who can advise you about your issue or situation. They do not like falsehoods or conversation fluff and will hit directly at the core of the matter. Alternatively, you should approach your situation from a lens of logic and truth to devise a plan of action.

A long-tailed skipper paused before she started grading her stack of papers from her Freshman English Composition class. She knew some would be terrible. There were always those students who refused to listen and had no desire to improve their writing. Some would be excellent. There were always those students who did not need a teacher, but a mentor instead to guide them down their writing path.

Then there would be some that had improved. There were always those students who absorbed her lectures and in-line critiques of their writing and applied their newfound knowledge. That is what she lived for, those moments when she could see that a student had grasped and understood the concept she had shown them.

Being an active participant in someone's growth as a writer is what made her heart sing. She took hold of her red pen and started reading the top paper from her stack. Which of the three would this one be?

Thoughts for Deeper Interpretation

Where could you use more-logical truths in your life?
If you cannot think of someone who could give you the logical advice you
    seek, how can you be that person for yourself?
In what ways can cutting directly to the truth of the matter aid you?

King of Swords

KEY IDEAS
Intelligent, logical, fair, lawmaker, counselor, strategist, warrior.
There's a man of intelligence and power in your life: father,
husband, teacher, et al. Sometimes he helps with advice or
protection or something else along those lines. Other times he is
an uncompromising authoritarian. Alternatively, you face a very
challenging situation that forces you to compromise yourself.

One night, after winning another case, a purple emperor sat reflecting on how far he had come since law school, when the judge knocked on his door.

"My apologies for arriving unannounced," said the judge.

"It is an honor, I assure you," the purple emperor responded. "May I get you something to drink?"

"No, I won't be long. What would you say your judicial philosophy is?"

"I would say I would follow these principles: First, always be prepared. Next, maintain an open mind while all sides present their issues. Also, treat all who appear in my court with dignity and respect. Fourth, afford all parties the same level of fairness. Last, have no personal agenda and uphold the rule of law."

The judge nodded, thanked the purple emperor, and left. The next day, it surprised the butterfly to hear the judge announce his retirement. But that feeling did not touch him when he settled onto that judge's bench a few months later.

Thoughts for Deeper Interpretation

Is the purple emperor someone you know, or is it you?

Where in your life could you use the purple emperor's fair and logical energy?

What lessons does the purple emperor have for you?

Wands

Ace of Wands

KEY IDEAS
inspiration, new goal, beginnings, potential, opportunity

A Weidemeyer's admiral butterfly despaired as a mining company paid the local people to cut down the forest surrounding their home. He didn't blame the people. Not really. They had to eat somehow. The mining corporation, on the other hand . . .

But how did one combat the power of capitalism?

It seemed impossible. The butterfly flew sadly through the remaining trees that towered above. Their memories stretched back centuries. What would the trees say to their children if they had the chance? But the butterfly didn't see any saplings.

That's when the idea exploded like an igniting star inside his brain: a charity that paid people to plant trees! Could such a thing work? It had to. He raced home to start researching how to get it done.

Thoughts for Deeper Interpretation

What new opportunities have come your way?

Where do you find your inspiration?

How can you ignite that passionate spark?

2 of Wands

KEY IDEAS
choosing between what's practical and
what you're passionate about

A red lacewing applied to art school as a joke. At least, that's what she told herself as she moved on to the college applications her parents had strongly encouraged her to fill out. Besides, the art school was just a backup in case the sensible colleges didn't want her as an incoming freshman. They would have art classes she could take as electives.

She did not anticipate getting accepted into art school and her parents' top college pick. How could she choose? Her parents insisted she go to the one they had picked out. It wasn't their life to live, though, was it? She had to decide between following her passion or going down the practical path.

Thoughts for Deeper Interpretation

How would you define passion and practicality?

What would happen if you pursued your passions? Describe the best- and worst-case scenarios.

Is there a way for you to balance both your passion and your practical side, and what would that look like?

3 of Wands

KEY IDEAS
active waiting, patience, foresight, successful enterprise

A Polydamas swallowtail covered the last seed she had planted with dirt. Soon, corn, soybeans, and wheat would begin sprouting, and she'd have an idea of what her harvest might look like. Ideally, the entire field would turn green in the next couple of weeks. If it stayed brown, however, that would mean she had failed.

Yet, there was nothing to be gained by standing at the edge of her field and anxiously rubbing her forelegs together. Instead, she flew off and checked over the equipment she would need for the eventual harvest. Her wheelbarrow had an issue with its wheel, so it was good she took the time to check.

Next, she invested in some animals, just in case her crops did fail. By diversifying, she ensured that she would, at worst, only go hungry in the winter instead of starving. Even though all of this kept her busy, she checked the field every day so she would be ready to catch those first sprouts.

Thoughts for Deeper Interpretation

When problems arise, what can you do to keep yourself calm?

What are some things you can do to make the process smoother?

Active waiting is like how in sports a player readies themselves to receive a passed ball. In your situation, how can you ready yourself to receive the successful end result?

4 of Wands

celebration, successful completion, harvest, relaxation

A lesser purple emperor decided to get into the sunflower business to give his caterpillar brood a better life. That summer, while planting and watering the sunflowers, he lost track of the number of blisters he popped. His efforts were not in vain, however, and the tall flowers gave seeds that fell like rain.

Not only would he make enough to last them through the winter, but he could afford to double the plants and thus the yield for the next summer. With his brood old enough to help, they should easily be able to handle the work involved.

That night after the harvest, the lesser purple emperor raised banners in celebration as he and his family feasted and danced until the sun rose.

Thoughts for Deeper Interpretation

What harvest are you ready to celebrate?
How can you replicate this kind of success going forward?
Who helped you and needs to be acknowledged in the celebration?

5 of Wands

An adopted bronze copper and brown veined-white grew up together as brothers. One day, their mother told them to collect some firewood. The bronze copper said, "I bet I can get more than you."

"Nah, bro, I got this," the brown veined-white said and flew off. The bronze copper went to work collecting sticks and soon had a nice pile. While searching for more little bits of wood, he heard a snapping sound. Frowning, the bronze copper winged over to see the brown veined-white snapping his sticks in two.

"Cheater!"

"Nothing against it in the rules."

The bronze copper decided not to waste time arguing and smashed a fist into the brown veined-white's mouth. The veined white stumbled back and picked up a stick. The bronze copper gritted his teeth, armed himself with a stick, and charged.

Thoughts for Deeper Interpretation

How do you keep yourself from crossing lines when angry with someone?
Why do you think siblings or roommates bother each other the most?
What healthful competitive outlets are available to you?

6 of Wands

As a caterpillar, the orange sulphur watched the Olympics and dreamed of one day flying a marathon and winning a gold medal. As soon as she emerged from her chrysalis, she began to train, for nothing was ever gained by mere dreaming.

Day after day, mile after mile, she flew, straining her wings, which screeched in pain as she pushed herself to fly faster and start winning races. Finally, after years of training, she qualified for the race.

The stadium cheered as she and the other racers crossed the finish line. And when the fans' voices deafened her as they draped the gold medal around her neck, it tasted sweeter than anything she had ever dreamed.

Thoughts for Deeper Interpretation

What does success look like to you?

Is receiving this good news how you imagined it would be?

If you need to boost your self-confidence, try looking in the mirror and giving yourself a high five. Compliment something about your appearance like you would a stranger. Tell yourself "good job" for getting through the day so far. Repeat daily as needed.

7 of Wands

The Sierra green sulphur had just landed on his favorite hilltop when the ants attacked. Wielding seven wands, they swarmed up the hill screaming, "This belongs to us now!"

He spread his wings wide and wrested a wand from the nearest ant.

"Leave now," he warned the ants. Ignoring him, they kept climbing and brandishing the remaining wands. With narrowed eyes, he took to the air and attacked. What chance did the ants have?

Thoughts for Deeper Interpretation

What obstacles are you overcoming?

Where could you dig in instead of running away?

Which conflicts in your life are worth fighting and which are worth running away from?

8 of Wands

An arctic skipper had entered a race. For months he woke before dawn to fly around the forest. This year he'd managed to shave thirty-seven seconds off his best 5-kilometer time, sixteen seconds shy of the forest record.

Nerves made his heart skip and his stomach twist the day of the race, but he had long since learned to channel that into his performance for a boost in speed. He queued up at the starting line with the other racers, and when the flag dropped, he flew off.

That's when a human started up a leaf blower. The fierce, artificial wind scattered butterflies and leaves alike. It was impossible to fight the rushing air, so the arctic skipper coasted on it and hoped it would take him across the finish line.

Thoughts for Deeper Interpretation

How can you ride or surf the events moving right now?

Are these forces anything you can influence, or are you simply swept up in them?

Is there anyone you can hold on to to avoid getting blown away?

9 of Wands

An American copper butterfly wanted to build a fence to protect its favorite flower. Things went fine until a human caught sight of the butterfly. Possibly entranced by the butterfly's orange shine, the human grabbed hold of her wings.

The butterfly flapped in a frenzy, and pain ripped through her wings. Suddenly, she popped free and she flew as fast as she could manage. The human tried to catch her, but she managed to flit away and find a pile of dead leaves to hide in.

While waiting for the human to leave, she examined her wing. Two empty gaps dissected the right wing. She slowly fanned her wing back and forth. It hurt, but the pain would ease in time. She could still fly.

Once the sky cleared, she went back to her unfinished fence. She struggled to lift the posts, but she would finish what she started. After all, the human could come back anytime, and she needed to be ready for when they did. Straining her wings, she got to work.

Thoughts for Deeper Interpretation

When else in your life have you had to push through an injury?
What does "resilient" mean to you, and can you imagine describing yourself
   in that way?
How can you motivate yourself to carry on?

10 of Wands

KEY IDEAS
A burden we wish we didn't have to carry.
Extra responsibility, hard work, completion, oppression.

The partner of a Queen Alexandra's birdwing had fallen ill, and no medicine they tried would cure them. However, butterflies whispered of a sunflower who knew not a butterfly's touch at the top of a hill, whose nectar could cure any ailment if you paid a toll in sticks.

There were reasons why no butterfly had landed on its petals.

The sticks were large and heavy. No other butterfly could hope to lift them. But her species was the largest of the butterflies, and she had no other options available to her. She took hold of a stick and flapped her wings. Slowly, she began to rise.

Not even a third of the way up the hill, her wings began to ache like a human had grabbed hold and begun to pull. But she kept going until they reached the top and deposited the stick at the sunflower's base. Then she went back to the ground for the next one.

Thoughts for Deeper Interpretation

Don't be afraid to ask for help when feeling overwhelmed and burdened. Who in your support system can you call? If there's no one, then reach out to a professional. Please.

What would it look like if you imagined tying balloons to the end of your burdens and then popped the balloon of the one you needed to hold at that very moment?

How could you take care of yourself today?

Page of Wands

KEY IDEAS
Inspiration and discovery. A messenger reminding you about what inspires you or fuels your passion. Or they may help you find what that is.

A fiery skipper liked a garden in front of a daycare. A little boy noticed the butterfly, and soon they made sure to smile at one another every morning. One day, the little boy smeared tears across his face when he arrived. Concerned, the butterfly followed him inside.

Inside, the loud and chaotic jumble of children almost disoriented the butterfly, and he nearly got stepped on twice. Thankfully his speed saved him, and it did not take him long to find the little boy. He sat at a table with untouched colored pencils and paper in front of him, his lips turned down and hands covering his cheeks and eyes.

The butterfly flitted onto the paper.

"How did you get in here?" the little boy asked.

The butterfly flew through a dollhouse door.

"Oh."

Then the butterfly hovered over a frowning face on a sign.

"Mommy said my pictures weren't real enough, and now I don't know what to draw."

With a nod, the butterfly winged back over and pushed a crayon toward the boy before posing on the edge of the paper. The boy's eyes went wide and he nodded. He gripped the colored pencil tightly and pressed it to the paper.

Knight of Wands

KEY IDEAS

A protector of energy and passion. He's impulsive, and his quick and adventurous nature can get him into trouble. Know anyone like that? If not, then channel these qualities into your situation.

A Milbert's tortoiseshell sat puddling on a shield with carved dragon scales outside an arcade when a crying salamander walked by.

"What's wrong?" the butterfly asked.

"I finally had enough money to rent the foosball table, but there's no one to play with."

"I'll play with you."

"Really?"

The butterfly nodded and flew inside the arcade. To the salamander's delight, they spent an hour in fierce competition. Then another player arrived, eager to participate in the fiery game.

The butterfly immediately winged aside.

"Don't you want to finish the game?" the salamander asked.

"I never wanted to play, only to make you smile," the butterfly said and took flight. The salamander's "Thank you" followed the smiling butterfly out of the arcade and into the sky to search for others to aid and protect their passions.

Thoughts for Deeper Interpretation

Is there someone protecting your passionate energies? If not, can it be you?

How could you follow your impulses without getting into trouble?

Queen of Wands

KEY IDEAS

Creative, generous, vibrant, strong. A very supportive and powerful woman has entered your life, and she happily shares her talents and skills. She wants to help, whether that be financially or creatively. However, she can also be overbearing and stir up chaos around her. Alternatively, it could be that you need to develop these qualities in yourself.

One day, an orange barred sulphur noticed a wilted and drooped sunflower under an eave.

"What saddens you?" she asked the sunflower.

"I cannot find the sun."

"Then I will borrow one of the sun's rays," she said and flew off before the sunflower could laugh at her foolishness. She landed on the rooftop and faced the sun.

"May I please borrow one of your rays for a sunflower?"

"Closer," the sun answered. Nodding, the butterfly flew until the sun's rays began to burn its body.

"Enough," the sun said and brushed a fingertip down the butterfly's thorax. The burning pain vanished, and fiery light began emanating from inside the butterfly.

"Thank you," she said to the sun and flew down to land on the sunflower.

"Sun? Is that you?" the sunflower asked as he began to straighten for the first time in his life.

"No, I am just a butterfly who has returned as promised," she said and poured the sun's power directly into the sunflower. All around them, sunflowers popped out of the ground and faced the butterfly as they grew. Laughing, the orange barred sulphur let go and danced among the flowers.

Thoughts for Deeper Interpretation

Is there someone offering to help you? This may be the time to take her up on it.

How could you embody the Queen's fiery and flamboyant energy in your situation?

In what ways can you help someone, or yourself, ignite their creative fire?

King of Wands

KEY IDEAS

Entrepreneur, vision, passionate ideas, a natural leader, advisor. This man can be a charismatic or visionary leader in your life, or possibly this is a role you need to step into. This card can also mean looking for a consultant or someone to guide you as you make your passion a reality.

A goatweed leafwing ignored the young, trembling butterfly sitting on the other side of the desk and focused on the business proposal in front of him. While the goatweed normally insisted that his clients be out of the chrysalis longer than a day before he saw them, the idea to open a trading-card shop that also sold cotton candy and popcorn had sparked his caterpillar-like excitement of running to the card shop as soon as he got his allowance.

However, this trembling butterfly who had yet to meet the goatweed's eyes was not ready for investment, no matter how strong the proposal was. With a sigh, the goatweed closed the folder. The younger butterfly jumped and the goatweed shook his head.

"Have you ever worked in a card shop?"

"No, but I spent every minute I could in one as a caterpillar."

"It is a very different experience being on the other side of the checkout counter. Come back when you have at least two years of experience working behind the counter."

The younger butterfly's disappointment did not faze the goatweed. Passion can take you only so far. Still, he hoped the younger butterfly would come back after gaining the needed experience to make their dream work.

Thoughts for Deeper Interpretation

How can you channel the King's energy into your situation?

Whom can you ask for entrepreneurial advice?

Where are the natural leaders in your life?

Ace of Cups

KEY IDEAS
love, compassion, creativity, healing, intuition, abundance, new beginnings

A painted beauty could not understand why her girlfriend loved her. After saying this, she expected her girlfriend to comfort her and recite a list of reasons why, as most usually did. But her girlfriend instead shook her head sadly.

"It is not my job to make you love yourself."

"Whose job is it?"

"Yours."

"But how do I do that?" the painted beauty asked as she tried to keep the tears inside. Her girlfriend softened and pulled her in for a comforting embrace. "You know. Spa days. Therapy. Meditation. All those kinds of things."

Afterward, the painted beauty got to work. She scheduled an appointment with a therapist and then one at the salon to get the tips of her forelegs painted. Then, she settled on a nice twig in the sun to meditate.

In her mind's eye, she saw a caterpillar, herself, crying.

"What's wrong?" she asked.

"You have forgotten to drink from the cup," the caterpillar answered.

"What cup?"

"This way," the caterpillar said and led the butterfly deeper inside her mind to stand in front of a cup with water spilling over its silver sides. The caterpillar pointed at the cup and said, "Drink."

The butterfly did so. Clear, pure love filled her body, and the cup continued to overflow no matter how much water she swallowed.

Thoughts for Deeper Interpretation

There are many different kinds of love; which kind do you think you are lacking, and how can you prepare yourself to receive it?

What steps can you take to help hear the voice of your inner child?

Where do you think new love comes from?

2 of Cups

KEY IDEAS
mutual attraction, partnership, new love, new interest or hobby

One day, as an elf butterfly worked as a mechanic, a *Delias argenthoa* walked into his shop. She was so shy and quiet that she could barely tell him what was wrong with her car. He spread his wings wide to shield her from the world. Finally, she smiled and reached out to hold his forelegs.

"Thank you," she said. His mouth dry, he could only nod as she explained that her car had started struggling to start. Right away he got to work. Most customers waited inside his office, but not her. She kept close to him the entire time.

Light conversation flowed between them like water trickling through a creek as he worked. Too soon, he fixed her car. She paid, blushed, and smiled. Indecision froze him. She was a customer, was she not? But a butterfly like that didn't fly by every day. Then she got in her car.

"Wait—you forgot something," he said before she could close the door. Her eyes fluttered in confusion, but she got out of the car. He pulled her in a hug, and when her cheek got close, he went to give her a small peck there. At the last moment, she turned her head and met him with a kiss of her own.

Thoughts for Deeper Interpretation

Is there someone you are interested in, and have you verified that they feel the same for you as you do for them?

What is something you can do to make yourself worthy of such love?

Sometimes new hobbies and interests can lead us to new people. Have you wanted to try something new? Now would be the time to put yourself out there!

3 of Cups

An archduke butterfly decided to throw a party to simply celebrate life and being alive.

"Would you like to come?" she asked her two closest friends.

"Of course! We'd be delighted to," they answered. "How can we help?"

"I need to clean, prepare drinks, and decorate," the archduke butterfly said. Soon all three were at the archduke butterfly's tree, and together they swept the branch, filled three cups with nectar, and blew up balloons, which they tied all around. Once they were ready, they raised their glasses to toast life.

Thoughts for Deeper Interpretation

When did you last celebrate something with your friends?

A celebration doesn't have to be something big like a party. What is something small that you and your friends could do?

Is there a project of yours that might benefit from collaboration?

4 of Cups

KEY IDEAS
dissatisfaction, depression, boredom, apathy,
reevaluation, contemplation

A common crow butterfly sipped from an attractive flower's nectar. It tasted sour, and only hunger's pangs stopped him from spitting it out. He shook his head and flew off to the next flower. But disappointment followed him there.

"This meadow has soured all its flowers," he said and took wing to search for sweet-tasting flowers. However, the disappointment continued to shadow his every wingbeat. The farther he flew, the more sour the flowers tasted.

Thoughts for Deeper Interpretation

Are you inadvertently coloring everything with your dark cloud? If so, what is something you can do to change your perspective?

If you suspect you might be suffering from depression, please see a professional.

What is something you can do to change your boredom and apathy into excitement and joy?

5 of Cups

KEY IDEAS
disappointment, grief, regret, mourning,
focusing on the negative

A mourning cloak butterfly laid her eggs at the base of a willow tree's leaf. Dehydrated, she flew off to a puddle to quench her thirst. On her way back, she passed a fly coming from the same leaf where her eggs rested.

Her wings beat with dread as she hurried back to what remained of her egg clutch. The ravenous fly had decimated her brood by eating nearly all of them. Hot tears dripped from her eyes and onto the leaf. The few eggs that had survived offered her little comfort for the losses she had suffered that day.

Thoughts for Deeper Interpretation

Hugs. I know that things are hard for you right now. What is a little thing that you can do for yourself right now? If it is only lying there and crying, that's okay.

Whom can you reach out to right now so you aren't alone?

What is something you are grateful for right now? Even if it is something basic, such as water to drink, take a moment to express gratitude for something.

6 of Cups

One day, a therapist asked a depressed *Hypochrysops theon* to describe a happy memory.

"I don't have any since I hardened into a chrysalis."

"So tell me about a time you were happy as a caterpillar," the therapist said. The butterfly thought for a while, silent seconds ticking by while he flipped through the pages of his life. Finally, he found a good one.

"I grew up on an oak leaf basket fern. We had plenty of food, and we thought we had shelter from predators. Anyway, I crawled to the edge of a leaf and looked down at the mottled brown dirt broken by greens of moss and saplings, with sprinkles of flowers adding pops of colors. Then the predators came and . . . that was the last time I was happy."

"Thank you for sharing that. When you get home, I want you to write that memory down. Then, whenever you feel sad, you can read and remind yourself of your past happiness."

"Whatever," the butterfly said and left the therapist's office. When he got home, thinking to prove the therapist wrong, he did as instructed. Except it worked.

Thoughts for Deeper Interpretation

What happy memories from your past are you remembering?
How could you recapture some of your childhood innocence?
When was the last time you got in touch with your inner child?

7 of Cups

KEY IDEAS
imagination, wishful thinking, choices, dreams and desires, illusion

While a chrysalis, an Indian leaf butterfly slipped into meditation. Seven cups sat before him, each holding a different flower: a lotus, hyacinth, sunflower, petunia, tulips, viola, and love-in-a-mist. All were what would come into his life when he took wing as a butterfly.

He knew, too, that he could not carry all of them throughout his life. While some, such as the purple hyacinth, would be forced upon him, others, such as the sunflower and tulip, could not be held together, and he would have to choose. But not yet. He still had time to enjoy all the glittering cups before emerging from the chrysalis.

Thoughts for Deeper Interpretation

Take time to examine the choices before you and see which are real and which ones are daydreams or illusions.

Which of your cups do you have to carry, and which can you let go?

8 of Cups

KEY IDEAS
disappointment, dissatisfaction, abandonment, doubt, leaving the past behind, decline

***

A gaudy commodore fluttered into a coffee shop.

"Welcome to Starla's Coffee! What can I brew fresh for you today?"

"Large dark roast with two creams and two sugars, please. And I'd like to pay for the person behind me."

"Absolutely. You're so kind!"

"Not at all. I just got a new job and want to share my fortune with others."

"Thank you, and please come again!"

***

"Welcome to Starla's Coffee! What can I brew fresh for you today?"

"Medium dark roast, please."

"Will that be all today?"

"I guess."

"New job still going well?"

"I guess."

"Thank you and please come again."

***

"Welcome to Starla's Coffee! What can I brew fresh for you today?"

"How much for a small cup of plain coffee?"

"Just a dollar. Are you all right?"

"I quit my new job this morning."

"But you were so excited!"

"The waters tasted bitter there. Time to see what's over the next hill."

"Good luck! Thank you and please come again."

Thoughts for Deeper Interpretation

How have you moved on after a disappointment in the past, and how has it influenced your current situation?

What does it take for you to abandon something in decline, and do you think that's a healthful boundary? If it's not, what can you do to change that?

Is there something in your life that you need to let go of so you can move on to something better?

---

9 of Cups

KEY IDEAS
satisfaction, achievement, wishes coming true,
financial or material success

A redspot sawtooth worked on writing a book for ten years. A sentence here on lunch at the office, a sentence there in the car line while picking her children up from school, and even a sentence at night while everyone slept.

Was it love or obsession driving her? She didn't know, but she did know that she had to get her story onto the page one little bit at a time. After writing "The End" came the editing, querying, and submission process, which took the same amount of time. Then after twenty years, she finally held her book in her forelegs.

The subsequent accolades and financial windfall were amazing, but they were not what sustained her as she started working on a new story. The dream, the wish, to see her book on other people's shelves, drove her to put one sentence down after another.

Thoughts for Deeper Interpretation

What wish have you started working on to make a reality?
What will you do once you have achieved your dream?
What does success look like to you?

10 of Cups

KEY IDEAS
harmony, happiness, contentment, alignment, healthful relationships, comfort, joy

It is the dream and life's work of many a biologist to revive an extinct species. In this story, one Jamaican biologist grew up with tales her great-grandmother told of a day-flying moth with bright, colored wings that filled the air with fluttering rainbows—the Sloane's urania, its last reported sighting in 1895, although it possibly survived until 1908.

Every rainbow's storm made her ache to witness those fluttering wings, a sight she wanted not just for herself, but for her future children. She worked through years of school and years of research before her first, failed attempt.

There were many others to follow. Still, she persisted. The year she gave birth to her first child coincided with the year the first Sloane's urania emerged from an egg in over 130 years. Years of work still lay ahead, but before her dark-skinned daughter turned eighteen, they traveled to Jamaica. Together, they released the day moths and gasped with delight in the fluttering rainbows just as her great-grandmother had done before.

Thoughts for Deeper Interpretation

What does a happy home mean to you?
How can you work to align yourself with your higher purpose today?
Where can you find contentment and happiness?

Page of Cups

KEY IDEAS

Youthful enthusiasm for something new, a message from the unconscious, a dream, or divination. An artistic youth will appear who will deepen your understanding of life through compassion or intelligent sensitivity (or both). Alternatively, you may need to begin a new compassionate service project or creative endeavor.

A blue moon butterfly slammed the paintbrush down and turned his back on the blank canvas. Another day of no progress. Frustrated, the butterfly lay down to take a nap. In his dreams, a caterpillar appeared and beckoned the butterfly to follow.

They traveled to a nodeweed plant that humans had smashed. The butterfly shuddered in horror, but the caterpillar did not stop and lifted one of the leaves. There, one egg had survived.

The caterpillar motioned toward the egg, and the butterfly winged over and gently picked it up. Once again the caterpillar began to move, and the butterfly followed it to a different nodeweed plant, this one protected by entwined branches. Carefully the butterfly placed the egg under a leaf.

Nodding, the caterpillar faded away, leaving the butterfly alone with the egg. He woke, then, and flew straight to his paints. The passing hours had no meaning to him as he painted the dream's compassionate image.

Knight of Cups

KEY IDEAS
A protector of romance and emotions in general. He follows his heart and creative outlets. A charmer. If there is no one in your life like this who can aid you right now, imagine taking on these qualities in your situation.

One day while flying across campus to make it to class, a Madagascar yellow pansy spied a young woman discreetly sketching a young man. On the first day, the butterfly did not think anything of it, but on the seventh day, he flew down and landed at the edge of her paper.

"Why do you sit here drawing him?"

"I love him, but he belongs to another, and so my art is the closest I can come to holding his hand," she answered.

"I see," said the butterfly and flew off to learn more about the young man. He did have another's hand in his own, but while he held only hers, she slipped her hands into many others.

Naturally, the butterfly felt a duty to share this knowledge with the young man. After the explosive breakup, the butterfly waited a few days for the young man to calm his emotions. Then, the butterfly plucked a shark's tooth from a shield and carried it to the young woman.

"What's this?" she asked.

"To give you courage to pursue your desires," he said and dropped it in her hands. When she examined the tooth, he picked up the woman's sketch. She cried out and reached for the sketch, but he evaded her grasp. As expected, she gave chase. The butterfly dropped the picture at the young man's feet, then landed on a rose to enjoy the love story unfolding in front of him.

Thoughts for Deeper Interpretation

Who could the Knight be in your life?

What qualities of the Knight could you use more of right now?

Think of something you can use to represent the Knight. When you feel that you need his power, you can hold it and feel his energy flow through you like the shark's tooth.

Queen of Cups

There's a compassionate and emotionally stable woman in the your life who can help you with your situation. She brings maternal comfort and stability with her as well. If there is no such woman, then maybe you need to channel these qualities in yourself.

A procilla beauty butterfly held her sobbing daughter. If the mother could wipe away her daughter's pain as easily as she could brush tears off a cheek, she would. But a parent can do only so much for their child, no matter how much they might wish otherwise. The daughter shuddered.

"I don't know what to do, Momma. He cheated."

The procilla beauty stomped down the swelling impulse to slash his wings. Her daughter did not need that. Instead, she continued to hold her child and said, "Take some time to process all these emotions. You don't want to make any decisions until your head is clearer."

"Okay. I can do that. How much time?"

"As long as your heart needs. It will depend, too, on what he did. There is a difference between a drunken mistake and an affair coated in lies. Either way, when your heart is ready, it will tell you what you need to do."

Her daughter nodded, then stopped and sank into herself again. "What if it tells me I'm still in love with him?"

"Do you love yourself?" the procilla beauty asked.

"Of course."

"Good. Then your heart already knows what you deserve from a loving partner."

King of Cups

KEY IDEAS
Compassionate, emotionally balanced, tolerance, emotional healing, wisdom. There is a man who can aid you at this moment. Possibly a counselor or other healthcare professional will offer aid for your greater emotional good. If there is no such person in the your life, perhaps it is time to seek one out.

A regal fritillary ignored the thick chart as he appraised the butterfly sitting on the other side of his desk. She kept her head down, her shoulders already defeated. He pushed the folder to the side and leaned forward.

"What brings you in here today?"

She sighed. "I tried to kill myself."

"Why?"

"You have my chart. The why is in there."

"I like to pretend with my patients that I am the first therapist they've ever seen. So. What brings you in here today?"

Her eyes flickered up at him. "They say my nonepileptic seizures are psychological, that they're in my head, which means it's my fault they happen, my fault I can't work, my fault for all of it."

He nudged the box of tissues on his desk toward her and then leaned back in his chair. "Who is 'they'?"

She sniffed. "Other doctors." Paused. "I don't know what to do."

"Have one," he said. Like he had slapped her, she reared back, her eyes meeting his for the first time.

"Excuse me?"

"Have a seizure. Right now. If it's all in your head and your fault, that means you can control them, right? So show me. Have one there on the couch. I legally can't tell anyone, so it doesn't matter."

"I've never tried that before," she said, confusion shaking the words that came out of her mouth. She closed her eyes and the seconds ticked by. Aside from her eyes pinching tighter, nothing happened. As he'd suspected.

"You can't, can you?" he said softly. She opened her eyes and shook her head. He eased himself forward toward her.

"None of this is your fault."

Tears sparkling with hope flooded her eyes.

Thoughts for Deeper Interpretation

Whom can you reach out to for tolerant compassion right now?

There are many magical techniques for healing emotional wounds. Which one feels right to you, and whom could you reach out to for guidance on it?

Do you have a therapist? How do you think talking to one would benefit you?

DISKS

Ace of Disks

KEY IDEAS
new beginnings, success, hard work, material abundance, security, health, financial or career opportunities, manifestation

A common green birdwing had an idea for a new business venture. His lover told him to follow his heart and that he would continue to stand next to him. His father walked him through how he could secure funding and where to find other resources for starting a small business. His mother, however, had different advice.

She pressed an orange seed into his forelegs and said, "The next full moon, plant this seed while you picture your business growing into success."

He knew not to question her and found himself digging in the dirt the next full moon. It took awhile for things to sprout, but with his determination, his lover's support, and his father's advice, as his mother's seed grew, so did his success.

Thoughts for Deeper Interpretation

Have you had a business idea? What steps can you take to make it a reality?

How can you prepare yourself for the hard work this new opportunity will require?

What can you do to welcome success into your life?

2 of Disks

A tiger swallowtail stared at the birthday invitation one of her caterpillars had brought home from school. She slid it over to her wife, who tapped it.

"Of course we would need to buy a gift the week you don't get paid and all our bills are due," she said and slid the invitation back to the swallowtail. Sighing, she stared at the party date and willed the numbers to change. When that didn't work, she opened her calendar on her phone to see the days when she had to pay each bill. And then she saw it, the answer.

"Do we still have a checkbook?" she asked. Her wife laughed.

"I haven't had to juggle bills like that in a while."

"True, but look, if we choose to mail this one in with a check instead of paying online . . ."

"We'll be good," the swallowtail said. They smiled and told the caterpillar to get ready to find the perfect gift. At the party, while the caterpillars played, the tiger swallowtail and her wife danced.

Thoughts for Deeper Interpretation

Have you focused too much lately on balancing the material and not celebrating your achievements?

What messages have you received lately, and do you think you have missed any underlying communication from the universe in them?

Could you be too focused on the obstacles and not be thinking about the potential benefits in your situation?

3 of Disks

KEY IDEAS
craftsmanship, teamwork, collaboration, partial completion of a work in progress

A gray hairstreak came across a pile of stones that made him pause. As a stonemason, he could tell that these stones not only would be fun to work with but would produce a beautiful result when carved and polished. However, he had no imagination and did not know what to carve out of the stones.

He searched galleries, farmers' markets, and co-ops until he found an artist who created dreamlike wooden sculptures that highlighted the wood's natural beauty. After examining every piece she had for sale, he handed her a picture of the stones.

"What would you do with this?" he asked. She studied the stones for several minutes before starting to sketch ideas on paper. Together, they decided on the design and fine-tuned it with her artistry and his knowledge of how stone worked. Once both of them were satisfied, he began to chisel the stone under her gaze.

Thoughts for Deeper Interpretation

Take a moment to evaluate the project you are working on. Do you need to make any adjustments? Now is the time to do so.

Whom can you reach out to and collaborate with on this project?

What skill of yours could you take time to develop?

4 of Disks

KEY IDEAS
gathering power, saving money or other resources, hoarding, stability

After almost starving over the winter, a gulf fritillary decided to gather what he could so he would never be that hungry again. That spring and summer, the butterfly worked to gather coins and nectar to last him through the winter.

Envious of the butterfly's hoard and convinced he had more than enough to make it through the frozen months, another butterfly decided to take a piece of the gulf fritillary's stash. The gulf fritillary easily swatted them with a stick, and the other butterfly just managed to crawl away with a broken wing.

However, this only increased the gulf fritillary's hunger and tightened the grip of his forelegs as he continued to grow his hoard.

Thoughts for Deeper Interpretation

Whatever you are holding on to, is it responsible saving or hoarding?
How does stability make you feel, and why?
What is driving you to gather or save at this time?

5 of Disks

KEY IDEAS
poverty, financial loss, not receiving needed help,
material needs, lack mindset

The snow came early that year, catching the spicebush swallowtail unprepared. Shivering, the butterfly took wing, in an attempt both to find shelter and to keep warm. Soon her body would shut down, and if it did before she found shelter, she knew she would not wake.

In the distance, she saw a flicker of light and flew toward it. A cathedral seemed to materialize out of the air as she flew closer to it. The hopeful lights danced behind stained glass, casting colored shadows onto the ground covered in white. Determination carried her to the front doors. She knocked. A black shadow, a man's outline, blocked the window's dancing colors.

She pressed her forelegs together, begging him to open the door. Maybe asking God might have been better, for he moved away from the window. Snow began to weigh down her wings as the door remained closed.

Thoughts for Deeper Interpretation

How do you approach financial loss?
What are different ways you could view your situation right now?
Hugs. Not having enough is hard. Is there anyone you could reach out to for aid whom you have not asked yet?

---

6 of Disks

KEY IDEAS
charity, generosity, giving and receiving, using abundance to benefit others

One day while flying, a wealthy amymone butterfly came across a butterfly crawling up a flower stem. Curious, the amymone swooped down to hover next to them and asked, "Why do you not fly?"

"Can you not see how a human ripped my wings?"

"My apologies, I did not look."

"No one does. If you don't mind, I am hungry and eager to reach the flower's nectar," the butterfly with tattered wings said. The amymone tried to bend a flower down to the other butterfly, but the stem held strong.

"It is hopeless," the crawling butterfly said.

"For this flower, yes. But come to the market. Hope is there," the amymone said and flew off to the nectar merchant at the nearest market. By the time the flightless butterfly arrived, the amymone had finished making the arrangements that would allow the other butterfly to have their fill of nectar, and the merchant would bill the amymone.

The butterfly with tattered wings ate his fill for the first time since the human attacked him, and he wept in gratitude.

Thoughts for Deeper Interpretation

How can you share your abundance?
What charity could you donate to at this time?
Whom can you practice generosity with today?

7 of Disks

A Colorado hairstreak inspected his grapevines. Most had plump, sweet, juicy grapes ready for picking. However, one section had damaged vines, and the grapes were small, scraggly, and sour. He frowned. His options were limited at this stage, but he refused to give up on those grapes.

He started working on healing the vine, and while it did recover and the grapes started to swell, they retained that sour taste. The other grapes sold for quite a profit, but the sour ones remained. He flew back and forth over them, tempted to throw them away, but not willing to discard the effort that had gone into them.

Then the simple answer came to him. He labeled them as "cooking grapes" and increased the price. They sold within an hour. Satisfied, he patted the vine and made plans to replicate the sour cooking grapes for the next year.

Thoughts for Deeper Interpretation

What do you see the results of your current efforts being in a year? Five years?

Where could you make changes now to increase your final yield?

Taking what you've learned so far, how can you make future attempts more profitable?

8 of Disks

"There are no knots in cross-stitch," the guava skipper caterpillar's grandmother admonished as she examined the caterpillar's cross-stitch. The caterpillar had finished her first cross-stitch not ten minutes before, and her pride melted under her grandmother's stern gaze.

"And the masters make the back look like the front," the grandmother said in a kinder tone as she handed the canvas back to the caterpillar. Many would have expected the caterpillar to quit, but she did not.

After she became a butterfly, she continued to stitch while her friends were playing games or out drinking. The feel of steel sliding through the canvas, followed by the tug and purr of thread, made her smile like nothing else. Finally, she finished her study of stitches.

She placed her sampler in her grandmother's forelegs. Once again the critical eye examined her work, but this time it seemed to sparkle as her grandmother smiled. "My backs were never this clean. Well done."

Thoughts for Deeper Interpretation

What does mastery of your skill look like?

How can you balance discipline in your life?

Whom can you reach out to who will not only validate you but also push you to the next level?

9 of Disks

abundance, financial independence, personal satisfaction, success, enjoying the fruits of your efforts

This was not the malachite butterfly's first harvest, or the second, or the third. It was, however, the one that earned enough money to pay the last of her debts and set up a financial cushion to cover the years when harvests were poor.

So, the butterfly packed a bag and flew to the mountains to rest and enjoy the flowers they had not seen since they were a caterpillar. She returned in plenty of time for the next harvest, but she was not alone. Her lover followed, carrying seeds that she used to multiply the next harvest.

Thoughts for Deeper Interpretation

When did you last enjoy the results of your hard work?

What does financial independence look like to you?

How can you achieve personal satisfaction every day?

10 of Disks

KEY IDEAS
financial security, family, wealth, confidence, pride in past accomplishments, long-term success

A mother-of-pearl butterfly settled into a seat at the stadium. Her body would ache that afternoon, but a worthwhile price to pay to watch her youngest graduate from college.

"The last graduation we went to had shade," her husband murmured.

She chuckled. "If we have attended enough graduations to become critics, then we are blessed indeed."

"That's all because of you. I don't know how you managed as a working mom, but you did amazingly," he said and reached over to squeeze her hand.

"How could I have done anything without you by my side to help with the kids?" she asked and leaned against him.

"I love you too."

"And you still want a Mediterranean cruise now that I'm retired and we no longer have to pay tuition, right?"

"As long as I'm with you, I'm happy. But if I have a vote, then yes. Mediterranean cruise. Oh, here they come," he said and pointed as graduates began to fill the stadium. She smiled.

Thoughts for Deeper Interpretation

What do you take pride in?
How can you bring confidence into your situation?
What can you do today to set yourself up for long-term success?

Page of Disks

KEY IDEAS

Positive message, possibility, financial opportunity, manifestation, skill development. Watch for a youth bearing a message that might carry financial potential. At the very least, it will be positive. If not, maybe you can ask your inner child to deliver said message to your higher self.

An orange theope who did IT work found himself labeled redundant and was let go after a larger company swallowed the business he'd worked at for the last five years. He left the office and flew off through the city, dazed and without aim.

Eventually, his wings tired and he landed on a bench next to a playground. Caterpillars laughed as they played, while he frowned as he sat. After a few minutes, a caterpillar crawled up to him.

"It's a great day! Why are you sad?"

"I lost my job."

"You should be out looking for a new one instead of sitting here."

The butterfly groaned. "You're not wrong."

The caterpillar grinned. "Have you checked the wall over there?"

"What's on the wall?"

"A bunch of old carvings."

"Kid, that's not going to help me right now."

"Are you sure?"

The butterfly ran a foreleg over his face and glanced at the stone wall that bordered the back of the playground. Shaking his head, he turned back to the caterpillar. The child had vanished. He searched the playground, but he never saw them again.

The butterfly shivered and flew over to the wall. Somehow, an advertisement had gotten stuck in one of the carvings. It was for an IT position. He applied. And while he eventually submitted applications for over a hundred jobs, the one the caterpillar had led him to eventually became his career.

Thoughts for Deeper Interpretation

Where can you go to hear positive messages?

Think of a place you could go outside your normal routine that has the potential for surprising opportunities.

How can you position yourself to receive news about what you are manifesting?

Knight of Disks

KEY IDEAS
A protector of responsibility, utility, establishing oneself, hardworking, caution instead of haste. The slowest of all the Knight cards, this could be either a younger person in your life (not a child like a Page, but not an experienced adult either) or a sign that you need to nurture these qualities in your own life.

On a Friday night, a veined white skipper studied at her desk in her dorm.

"Come drink with me," their roommate said.

"Can't. Don't want to mess up my last semester."

Every day her roommate asked, and every day the veined white skipper answered the same. The next Friday, her roommate didn't ask and instead slid a beer across the veined white skipper's desk.

"That's not in the plan."

"You work too much," her friend said. The skipper glanced up. The beer had gone behind one of the skipper's action figures who held a shield of diamonds. After staring for several long moments, the skipper nodded.

"And you play too much," the skipper said. She slid the beer back, the sensible, cautious, and responsible choice, and turned back to finish the work in front of her so she could graduate with honors.

Thoughts for Deeper Interpretation

How could embodying the Knight's hardworking mindset aid your situation?

Where could you use more responsible caution in your life?

What would it take for you to feel established in your situation?

Queen of Disks

KEY IDEAS

Practical, nurturing, wisdom, attention to detail, efficient, making the most out of what you have. A nurturing woman, possibly a working mom, can aid you at this time. Her practical advice on how to make the best use of available resources can be particularly helpful at this time. Alternatively, it could be that you need to embrace that energy in your own life.

A common imperial blue tied off the final thread on a quilt. One day, her granddaughter would love it. As the butterfly folded the heavy blanket, her youngest daughter called.

"Hello?"

"Mom, guess what? No wait, don't. You won't get it. He asked me to marry him!"

"That's wonderful. You said yes, didn't you?"

"Of course I did. We've already started planning things, and I want you to make my wedding dress."

The butterfly, flattered, sank into a chair. "What did you have in mind?"

"Nothing much. Just a little hand beading. I'll send you some pictures. Love you, bye," her daughter said and hung up. Her phone dinged with messages. The butterfly groaned and rubbed her temples. All the gowns sparkled from hemline to sweetheart neckline. After a few minutes, the butterfly got up and checked the beads she had.

Her stash amounted to about a third of what she'd need for the dress, which saved her a significant amount of money. Every dime saved helped keep the wedding within budget. She worked on the gown daily but still had to finish the last few stitches the morning of the wedding.

"Next time you want something hand-beaded, you do it yourself," the butterfly said as she zipped her daughter into the wedding dress.

"Oh, Mom, it's perfect. Thank you."

Her daughter sparkled as she came down the aisle, drawing every eye to the beautiful bride.

Thoughts for Deeper Interpretation

Whom can you turn to for practical advice in your situation?

How could frugal thinking and using what you have aid you at this time?

What details could you examine closer that you may have overlooked?

King of Disks

Wealth, self-discipline, abundance, patron, efficiency, leadership, sales, investment. An older, established man is available to aid you, be it with financial advice or with a material investment of some kind. If not, then maybe you will be entering a financially stable time of your life by calling on this King's energy.

A Saturn butterfly eyed the new real estate agent hopeful who had just joined his brokerage. Though young, she had a hunger in her eyes he knew all too well.

"Welcome to my brokerage," he said.

"Thank you for having me. I am excited to get started."

"That's good, but let's pump the brakes a little bit. You will shadow me for a few months before I let you take the lead. The first year will be split commissions. After that year is up, we will evaluate your progress. How does that sound?"

"Good, sir."

"Excellent. Let's get started," he said and shepherded her into the meeting with her first client. It went well, as did the next several, and the first two she took the lead on. The third one walked away from the brokerage because of an error she made, but he used it as a learning experience. Dents in paychecks were the perfect punishments and motivators.

Even then, the light in her eyes stayed bright. At the end of the year, he stepped away from her with pride and said, "You're ready."

She bowed her head and held up a wrapped gift. "Thank you for your help and everything you've taught me."

He unwrapped it to reveal a crystal flower, and he kept it on his desk until he returned to the earth.

Thoughts for Deeper Interpretation

Where could you use more self-discipline in your life?

How can you be like the King and share your knowledge?

Whom can you look to for leadership and financial advice right now?

Healing Patterns and Prompts

Included here are several healing patterns for you to stitch if you feel called to do so. Again, cross-stitch and writing are two of many tools needed on any healing journey and are no substitute for professional help. Each design has both an advanced and beginner version of the pattern, but I hope that those of you who start with a beginning pattern will end with an advanced one.

Beginners, I have not included instructions on how to cross-stitch here, but I do have tutorials up on my YouTube channel (@starlayilmaz) for you to watch when it is convenient for you.

Advanced stitchers, there is one stitch on the Finding Balance design that you may not have run into before. It is a stitch I innovated specifically for this project, but if someone has seen it on an older project, please let me know. I am calling it an overstitch, and you can find a tutorial for it on my YouTube channel (@starlayilmaz).

Please feel free to share your stitches on social media and tag me! I can't wait to see what you make.

Finding Balance

 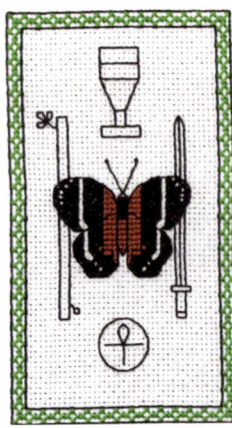

The banded peacock from the Justice card sits here, surrounded by the elements of the Minor Arcana. This design is about keeping the different elements of yourself in balance. For instance, I am a mother, writer, and cross-stitcher, among many other things. If I neglect myself as a mother in favor of the cross-stitcher, my life and my children's lives will be upended. While it can be challenging to find the right balance (and this is something that children have a very hard time understanding!), if the scales tilt far enough for long enough they will spill everything they are holding.

Writing Prompt

Identify the different parts of yourself and write out a conversation between them where they state what they need. Then, figure out a compromise between them so you can move forward in a more healthful and more balanced way.

THOUGHTS WHILE STITCHING

Am I out of balance, and if so, where?
What is one way to keep the different aspects of myself in alignment?
How can I address the parts of myself that I have neglected?

Finding Balance, Beginner Pattern

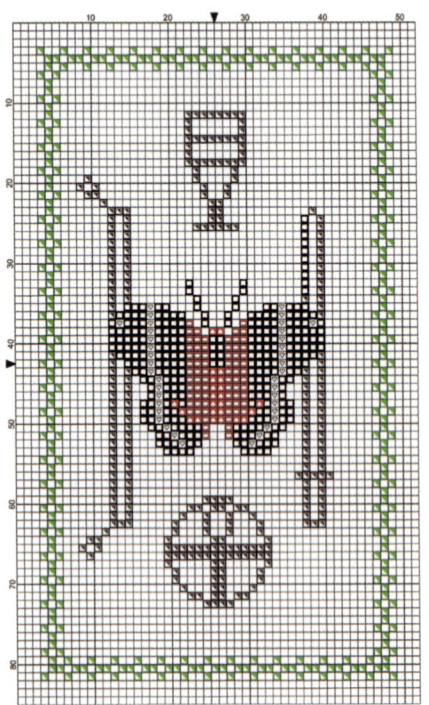

Legend:

☐ ■	DMC-310
◩	DMC-702
◪	DMC-White
◩	DMC-321
■	DMC-3721
◪	DMC-3799

Backstitches:
— DMC-310

Finding Balance, Advanced Pattern

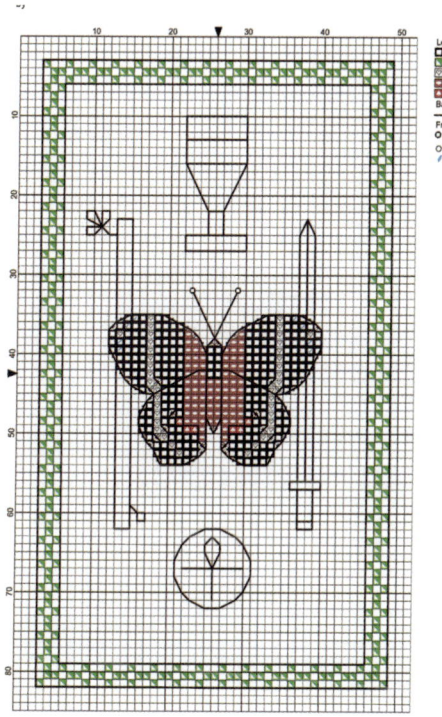

Showing Yourself Love

It is incredibly important to show ourselves love when we are in need of healing. This is often called self-care, but it is deeper than that. This butterfly, the *Callicore aegina*, comes from the 10 of Swords card, where the butterfly has been stabbed through its abdomen and pinned to a shelf. Often the 10 of Swords can mean being stabbed in the back, and it's in those moments where we need to give ourselves some love.

Writing Prompt

Describe what self-care looks like and how that differs from what you need to feel loved. There could be some overlap, and that's fine. Now go ahead and write what makes you feel loved. When you are finished, it might be a good idea to do something for yourself both from the self-care and self-love categories.

THOUGHTS WHILE STITCHING

Are there more similarities or differences between how I define self-care and self-love, and why might that be?

Daily, how do I practice self-care and show myself self-love?

What in my life prevents or tries to stop me from giving care and love to myself?

Showing Yourself Love, Beginner Pattern

Showing Yourself Love,
Advanced Pattern

You Are Strong and Powerful

The 9 of Wands shows us a butterfly with part of its wing missing who still has the strength to lift a wand. It's easy to forget our own strength and power when we have been injured and need to slow down and heal. Yet, the fact that we have survived this latest trauma is proof enough of our strength and power. Take pride in making it this far.

Writing Prompt

Write out different moments in your life when you have felt powerful. Then describe how those lessons can aid you now.

THOUGHTS WHILE STITCHING

How can you move forward in your life after this trauma?

When was the last time you gave yourself a high five for making it through the day? Why not do it now?

Is there a fictional character you could imagine stepping into your body and filling you with their strength?

You Are Strong and Powerful, Beginner Pattern

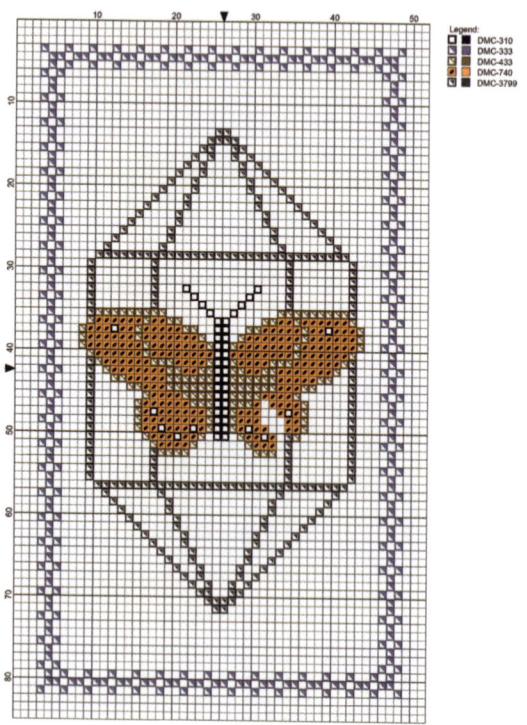

Legend:
DMC-310
DMC-333
DMC-433
DMC-740
DMC-3799

You Are Strong and Powerful, Advanced Pattern

Legend:
- ■ DMC-310
- DMC-333
- DMC-433
- DMC-740

Backstitches:
— DMC-310

French Knots:
○ DMC-310

Recommended Resources

Here are a few of the books and websites I found helpful on my Tarot journey. If you would like to explore further and deepen your relationship with Tarot, these are a good place to start.

Boyer, Janet. *Tarot in Reverse: Making Sense of the Upside Down Cards in a Tarot Spread*. Atglen, PA: Schiffer, 2012.

Cowles, Lynda. *The Tarot Playbook: 78 Novel Ways to Connect with Your Cards*. Atglen, PA: Schiffer, 2012.

Esselmont, Brigit. Biddy Tarot. https://biddytarot.com/.

Hammond, Eleanor. *A Course in Tarot: In-Depth Training, Exercises, Questions with Answers*. Atglen, PA: REDFeather Mind, Body, Spirit (Schiffer), 2018.

Labyrinthos. https://labyrinthos.co/.

Moore, Barbara. *Tarot for Beginners*. Woodbury, MN: Llewellyn Worldwide, 2010.

Oken, Alan. *Pocket Guide to the Tarot*. New York: Random House, 1996.

Place, Robert M. *The Tarot: History, Symbolism, and Divination*. New York: Penguin, 2005.

Pollack, Rachel. *Seventy-Eight Degrees of Wisdom: A Tarot Journey to Self-Awareness (a New Edition of the Tarot Classic)*. Newburyport, MA: Weiser Books, 2019.

Waite, Arthur Edward. *The Pictorial Key to the Tarot*. London: Rider, 1910.

Author Bio

Starla Yilmaz has been reading Tarot for over 20 years and has been cross-stitching even longer. An avid writer with numerous short publications, she is a two-time winner of the Prepublished Maggie Award for Excellence for her work in romantic fiction. When she's not busy creating worlds with words or thread, you might find her doing so while playing Minecraft. She lives with her family in Georgia.